W9-AQL-763

Date: 11/08/11

J 972 SEX
Sexton, Colleen A.,
Mexico /

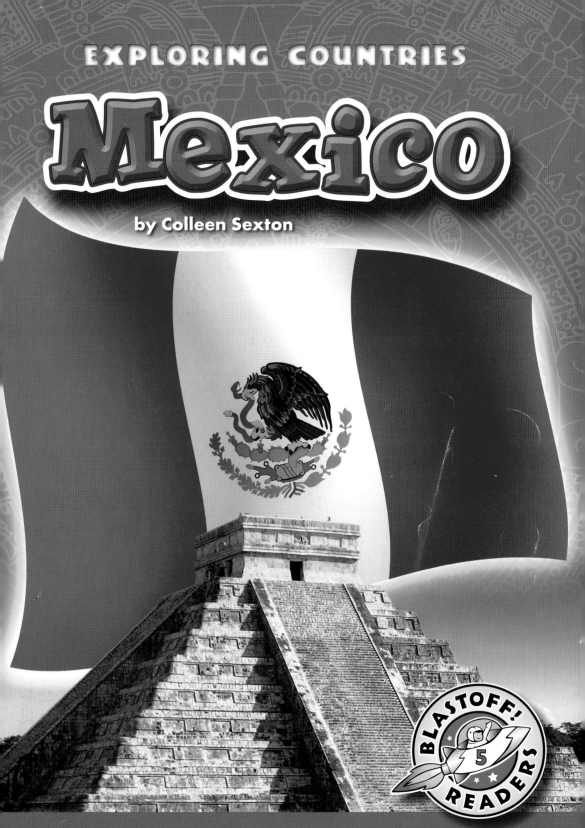

EXPLORING COUNTRIES

Mexico

by Colleen Sexton

BELLWETHER MEDIA • MINNEAPOLIS, MN

BLASTOFF! 5 READERS

Note to Librarians, Teachers, and Parents:

Blastoff! Readers are carefully developed by literacy experts and combine standards-based content with developmentally appropriate text.

Level 1 provides the most support through repetition of high-frequency words, light text, predictable sentence patterns, and strong visual support.

Level 2 offers early readers a bit more challenge through varied simple sentences, increased text load, and less repetition of high-frequency words.

Level 3 advances early-fluent readers toward fluency through increased text and concept load, less reliance on visuals, longer sentences, and more literary language.

Level 4 builds reading stamina by providing more text per page, increased use of punctuation, greater variation in sentence patterns, and increasingly challenging vocabulary.

Level 5 encourages children to move from "learning to read" to "reading to learn" by providing even more text, varied writing styles, and less familiar topics.

Whichever book is right for your reader, Blastoff! Readers are the perfect books to build confidence and encourage a love of reading that will last a lifetime!

This edition first published in 2011 by Bellwether Media, Inc.

No part of this publication may be reproduced in whole or in part without written permission of the publisher. For information regarding permission, write to Bellwether Media, Inc., Attention: Permissions Department, 5357 Penn Avenue South, Minneapolis, MN 55419.

Library of Congress Cataloging-in-Publication Data

Sexton, Colleen A., 1967-
  Mexico / by Colleen Sexton.
      p. cm. – (Exploring countries) (Blastoff! Readers)
  Includes bibliographical references and index.
  Summary: "Developed by literacy experts for students in grades three through seven, this book introduces young readers to the geography and culture of Mexico"–Provided by publisher.
  ISBN 978-1-60014-487-5 (hardcover : alk. paper)
  1. Mexico–Juvenile literature. I. Title.
  F1208.5.S49 2011
  972–dc22   2010019779

Printed in the United States of America, North Mankato, MN.

080110   1162

Contents

United States

Rio Grande

Baja California
peninsula

Mexico

Pacific Ocean

Mexico City

Did you know?

Mexico used to include a large
part of the western United States.
Mexico lost the land to the
United States at the end of the
Mexican-American War in 1848.

Mexico, the southernmost country in North America, spans
758,449 square miles (1,964,375 square kilometers) of
the **continent**. The United States lies across Mexico's
northern border. The Rio Grande, one of the longest rivers
in North America, flows for 1,250 miles (2,012 kilometers)
along this boundary.

Gulf of Mexico

Yucatán
Peninsula

Caribbean Sea

← Belize

↑
Guatemala

To the southeast, Mexico borders Belize and Guatemala.
The Pacific Ocean washes Mexico's western shore.
On the east coast, the Yucatán **Peninsula** separates the
waters of the **Gulf** of Mexico from the Caribbean Sea.
Mexico City is the country's capital.

Most of Mexico's cities lie on a large **plateau** in the middle of Mexico. In some places, this flat land rises more than 1 mile (1.6 kilometers) high. Rocky mountain ranges with snowy peaks surround the plateau. Mountainsides covered in forests slope down to meet rolling hills and plains. Beyond the plains, sandy beaches and **wetlands** line the coasts. In the northwest, the Baja California peninsula goes for long periods of time without rain. Deep canyons and rocky deserts cover much of northern Mexico. **Tropical rain forests** lie in the far south where the weather is hotter.

fun fact

Several of the world's most active volcanoes stand among Mexico's mountains. One of the largest is *Popocatépetl*, or Smoking Mountain. *Popo*, as Mexicans call it, puffs out smoke and ash.

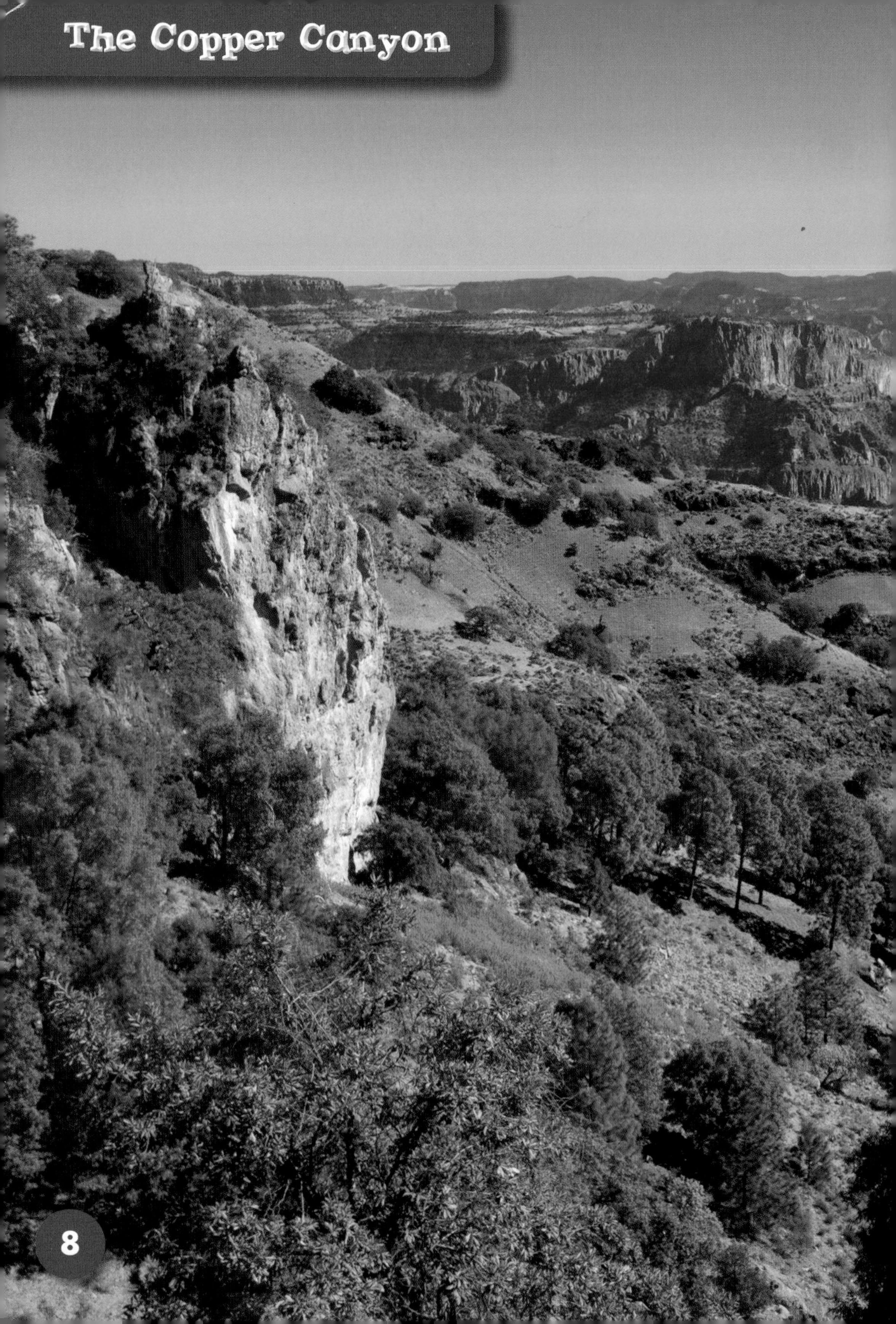

The Copper Canyon, or *Barranca del Cobre*, is the largest canyon system in the world. It stretches for more than 20,000 square miles (51,800 square kilometers) across northwestern Mexico. The Copper Canyon system has six main canyons and twenty canyons in all. They were carved by six rivers over thousands of years. The deepest canyons plunge at least 6,000 feet (1,830 meters). The Copper Canyon gets its name from the green color of the canyon walls. They look like aged copper.

fun fact

The most popular way to see the Copper Canyon is by train. For more than 400 miles (644 kilometers), trains follow a winding track that passes through 86 tunnels. One of the tunnels is more than 1 mile (1.6 kilometers) long.

iguana

quetzal

dahlia

! fun fact

The round, colorful dahlia is Mexico's national flower. Dahlias originally grew wild in the country's mountains. Today, they brighten gardens around the world.

Many kinds of animals and plants can be found in Mexico. In mountain forests full of pines, firs, and oaks, bears and mountain lions stalk their prey. Jaguars hunt in the rain forests. There, colorful birds like quetzals and parakeets fly from treetop to treetop.

jaguar

Coyotes roam among cactuses in the northern deserts.
The deserts are also home to Gila monsters, iguanas,
rattlesnakes, and other reptiles. Deer and rabbits nibble
on the grasses and shrubs of the central plateau.
Every December, thousands of gray whales migrate to
the coast of northwestern Mexico to give birth.

fun fact

The Mayans are the largest group of native peoples in North America. They have lived on Mexico's Yucatán Peninsula for thousands of years.

Most of Mexico's 112 million people are *mestizos*, or people of mixed race. They have European **ancestors** who first arrived from Spain in the 1500s. Their ancestors are also **native** peoples who were already in Mexico when the Spanish arrived. Native peoples make up the second-largest group in Mexico. Many wear **traditional** clothes and speak their own languages.

Mexico is also home to **immigrants** from countries in Europe, Asia, and North and South America. Almost all Mexicans speak Spanish, which is the country's official language.

Did you know?
Mexico has a young, fast-growing population. About half of all Mexicans are under 20 years old.

Speak Spanish!

Mexico is the largest Spanish-speaking country in the world! Here are some Spanish words for you to try.

English	Spanish	How to say it
hello	hola	OH-lah
good-bye	adiós	ah-dee-OHS
yes	sí	SEE
no	no	NOH
please	por favor	POHR fah-VOR
thank you	gracias	GRAH-see-uhs
friend (male)	amigo	ah-MEE-goh
friend (female)	amiga	ah-MEE-gah

Mexico City

fun fact

One out of every five Mexicans lives in Mexico City. The area in and around Mexico City has more than 20 million people. It is one of the largest cities in the world!

Most Mexicans live in large, crowded cities. They live in small, modern houses or in high-rise apartment buildings. Colorful **adobe** houses line the streets of older neighborhoods. People who live in poor areas crowd into small shelters made of scrap metal and wood. They do not have electricity or running water.

Where People Live in Mexico

countryside 23%

cities 77%

In the countryside, people live on farms or in small villages. Their adobe or stone homes usually have one or two rooms. Almost every city and village has a marketplace where people go to buy, sell, and trade food, clothes, and other goods. A visit to the marketplace is also a time to catch up with friends and neighbors.

Did you know?

Most Mexicans are Roman Catholic. A Catholic church can be found in nearly every city and small village. It is a central gathering place that is part of everyday life.

Mexican children start school when they are 6 years old. They must go to elementary school for six years and middle school for three more years. Students take classes in reading, writing, math, science, and history. In some schools, students study English or other languages. Students in Mexico do not have to attend high school. Some go to work instead to help support their families. Students who continue their education can choose between two different kinds of schools. Some high schools prepare students to go to college. Others offer training for specific jobs they can start after graduating.

fun fact

The National Autonomous University of Mexico was founded in 1551. It is almost 500 years old!

Working

About two out of every three Mexican workers have **service jobs**. They work in schools, banks, hospitals, and government offices. Service workers are important to Mexico's large tourist industry. People working in restaurants and hotels serve the millions of tourists who visit Mexican resorts and cities each year. Factory workers in Mexico City make about half of all goods produced in the country, including cars, food products, chemicals, and paper.

Did you know?

Factories called *maquiladoras* lie near Mexico's border with the United States. Workers in these factories make auto parts, clothing, electronics, and other goods for companies in the United States.

Where People Work in Mexico

services 62.9%

farming 13.7%

manufacturing 23.4%

! fun fact

Mexican artists are famous for their skill. They make pottery, handwoven blankets and baskets, and silver jewelry. Artists sell most of their goods to travelers from other countries.

In the countryside, Mexican farmers grow corn, coffee, lemons, chili peppers, and many other crops. In central Mexico, miners dig up silver and other **minerals**. These crops and minerals are sent all over the world.

Mexicans spend their free time with family and friends. Every city and village has a plaza, or public square, where people gather in the evening to relax. They listen to folk singers and lively *mariachi* bands, which feature violin, trumpet, and guitar players. On weekends, Mexicans eat big family meals at home or take picnics to public parks. Many Mexicans go to **bullfights** to cheer on the bullfighters, or *matadors*. The biggest crowds come out to watch soccer and baseball, which are called *fútbol* and *béisbol* in Mexico. Nearly every city, town, neighborhood, and school has its own teams.

luchador

fun fact

Lucha libre is professional wrestling in Mexico. *Luchadores* wear masks and colorful costumes in the ring. These wrestlers are famous for their high-flying moves that thrill crowds.

matador

Did you know?

Many Mexicans eat their main meal in the middle of the day. Some people also take time for a quick nap, or *siesta*, before going back to work in the afternoon.

enchiladas

posole

Long ago, the ancestors of modern Mexicans learned how to grow corn, or *maize*. Corn is still a main ingredient in many Mexican dishes. People have been making *posole*, a traditional corn stew, for over 1,000 years. *Tamales* are made with ground corn and pork or chicken. They are steamed inside corn husks and served hot.

Cooks also make ground corn into tortillas. They wrap these round, flat pieces of bread around a mix of meat and cheese to make snacks like tacos and *enchiladas*. Cooks spice up many dishes with chili peppers and use avocados, bananas, and papayas to add flavor. *Mole poblano* is Mexico's national dish. It is turkey or chicken topped with a spicy sauce called *mole*, made of chilies, chocolate, and nuts.

Most holidays in Mexico are celebrated with big parties, or *fiestas*. Almost every *fiesta* features music, dancing, fireworks, parades, and prayer. One of the biggest *fiestas* is the five-day celebration of *Carnaval* in the week before the Christian season of **Lent**. Christmas, Easter, and other Christian holidays are also important in Mexico.

On December 12, many Mexicans honor their **patron saint**, Mary, the mother of Jesus. They call her "Our Lady of Guadalupe."

The most important national holiday is Independence Day. It falls on September 16. Mexicans gather on plazas decorated with flags, flowers, and lights to celebrate their country's independence.

fun fact

At many *fiestas*, children play the *piñata* game. They take turns wearing a blindfold and using a long wooden stick to hit a colorful decoration hung high above their heads. When the *piñata* breaks open, everyone grabs the candy and toys that fall to the ground.

Did you know?

On the Day of the Dead, or *Día de los Muertos*, families celebrate the lives of loved ones who have died. Mexicans make altars to hold flowers, candles, and food for the dead.

Carnaval

Mexico is a land of contrasts. It is a mix of the old and the new. Among the busy, modern cities stand ancient ruins. Long ago, native peoples such as the Mayans and the Aztecs built cities with palaces, parks, and pyramids.

Chichén Itzá

The Mayan ruins of Chichén Itzá lie on the Yucatán Peninsula. The ruins include a stone pyramid with a temple at the top. The Aztec ruins of the ancient city of Tenochtitlán lie in Mexico City. Today, visitors can tour these ruins and explore Mexico's exciting past.

Fast Facts About Mexico

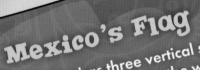

Mexico's Flag

The Mexican flag has three vertical stripes. The green stripe stands for hope, the white stripe stands for unity, and the red stripe stands for the blood of Mexico's heroes. The country's coat of arms is in the center of the flag. The current flag design has been used since 1821, but it was officially adopted in 1968.

Official Name: United Mexican States

Area: 758,449 square miles (1,964,375 square kilometers); Mexico is the 15th largest country in the world.

Capital City:	Mexico City
Important Cities:	Guadalajara, Ecatepec, Puebla, Ciudad Juárez, Tijuana, Monterrey, León
Population:	112,468,855 (July 2010)
Official Language:	Spanish
National Holiday:	Independence Day (September 16)
Religions:	Christian (82.8%), Other (17.2%)
Major Industries:	farming, fishing, manufacturing, mining, services, tourism
Natural Resources:	oil, iron ore, farmland, natural gas, fish, wood
Manufactured Products:	cars, food products, steel, chemicals, wood products, clothing
Farm Products:	corn, wheat, soybeans, rice, beans, cotton, coffee, fruits, tomatoes, beef, poultry, dairy products
Unit of Money:	peso; the peso is divided into 100 centavos.

Glossary

adobe—bricks made of clay and straw that are dried in the sun

ancestors—relatives who lived long ago

bullfights—sporting events in which people fight with and kill bulls; bullfights happen in bullrings.

continent—one of the seven main land areas on Earth; the continents are Africa, Antarctica, Asia, Australia, Europe, North America, and South America.

gulf—part of an ocean or sea that extends into land

immigrants—people who leave one country to live in another country

Lent—the forty days before the Christian holiday of Easter when Catholics fast

minerals—elements found in nature; gold, iron, and oil are examples of minerals.

native—originally from a place

patron saint—a saint that a group of people, or a country, looks to for protection and guidance

peninsula—a section of land that extends out from a larger piece of land and is almost completely surrounded by water

plateau—an area of flat, raised land

service jobs—jobs that perform tasks for people or businesses

traditional—related to the stories, beliefs, or ways of life that families or groups hand down from one generation to another

tropical rain forests—thick, green forests that lie in the hot, wet areas near the equator; it rains about 200 days each year in many tropical rain forests.

wetlands—wet, spongy land; bogs, marshes, and swamps are wetlands.

To Learn More

AT THE LIBRARY
Goulding, Sylvia. *Festive Foods! Mexico*. New York, N.Y.: Chelsea Clubhouse, 2008.

Landau, Elaine. *Mexico*. New York, N.Y.: Children's Press, 2008.

Philip, Neil. *Horse Hooves and Chicken Feet: Mexican Folktales*. New York, N.Y.: Clarion Books, 2003.

ON THE WEB
Learning more about Mexico is as easy as 1, 2, 3.

1. Go to www.factsurfer.com.

2. Enter "Mexico" into the search box.

3. Click the "Surf" button and you will see a list of related Web sites.

With factsurfer.com, finding more information is just a click away.

Index

The images in this book are reproduced through the courtesy of: Alex Garaev, front cover, pp. 26-27;
Maisei Raman, front cover (flag), p. 28; Juan Eppardo, pp. 4-5; Radius Images/Photolibrary, pp. 6-7;
Marco Regalia, p. 6 (small); Blaine Harrington III/Alamy, pp. 8-9; Danita Delimont/Alamy, p. 9 (small);
Wendy Shattil/Photolibrary, pp. 10-11; Scott Truesdale, pp. 10 (top), 23 (right); worldswildlifewonders,
p. 10 (middle); Kerry Vanessa McQuaid, p. 10 (bottom); Dallas & John Heaton/Photolibrary; Randy
Faris/Photolibrary, p. 14; Elena Elisseeva, p. 15; Blaine Harrington/Photolibrary, pp. 16-17; Ed Lallo/
Photolibrary, p. 18; David Coleman/Alamy, p. 19; AFP/Getty Images, pp. 20-21; George Koroneos, p.
20 (small); Peter Donaldson/Alamy, p. 22; Solaria, p. 23 (left); Miriam Reik/Photolibrary, pp. 24-25;
Danilo Ascione, p. 29 (bill); Chris Hill, p. 29 (coin).